The W&A, the *General*, and the Andrews Raid: A Brief History

Robert C. Jones

Robert C. Jones
P.O. Box 1775
Kennesaw, GA 30156

jone442@bellsouth.net
rcjbooks.com

"The W&A, the *General*, and the Andrews Raid: A Brief History", Copyright 2010 by Robert C. Jones. All rights reserved.

First Edition

ISBN: 1453751394
EAN-13: 9781453751398

This book is dedicated to Colonel James Bogle, for his dedication to preserving the history of the *General* and the Great Locomotive Chase.

Contents

Contents	4
Introduction	6
The Coming of the Western & Atlantic Railroad	8
Engineering obstacles	11
Construction	11
Organization	15
Facts and figures	16
Enter the General and the Texas	16
Civil War Years – 1861-1862	17
The Great Locomotive Chase	20
Aftermath	23
Retracing the Route of the Andrews Raid	25
Stop #1 – The Kennesaw House	25
STOP #2 - Kennesaw, Georgia	27
STOP #3 - Moon's Station	30
STOP #4 - Etowah River Bridge	32
STOP #5 - Cooper Furnace	35
STOP #6 - Cass Station	36
STOP #7 – Kingston	38
STOP #8 – Adairsville	40
Stop #9 – Calhoun	43
STOP #10 - Oostanuala River Bridge (Resaca)	45
Stop #11 – Dalton Depot	46
STOP #12 - Tunnel Hill	48
STOP #13 – Ringgold	50
Other Spots to Visit	53

Civil War – 1863-1865	57
Post-Civil War	70
The General	70
Reconstruction	71
The Great Kennesaw Route	72
The Century Turns	77
1962 Centennial Run of the General	80
Return of the General to Kennesaw	82
The General Stamp	90
The 21st Century	91
Appendix: Nashville, Chattanooga & St. Louis and beyond	93
Sources	96
The Author on YouTube	98
About the Author	99

Introduction

The ambitiously named Western and Atlantic Railroad (it never reached the Atlantic Ocean or anywhere west of Atlanta) ceased to exist in 1890, and at its peak commanded a main line only 137-miles long. Yet today, it is still one of the most easily recognizable names in the history of American railroading. Why? The W&A played an important role in two of the most famous incidents in the Civil War, including the Andrews Raid (a.k.a. Great Locomotive Chase) in 1862, and Sherman's Atlanta Campaign (1864), where it served as the Union supply line. This book will examine the brief but significant life of this famous railroad, as well as the history of its most famous locomotive – the *General*. The book also contains a step-by-step "Retracing the Route of the Andrews Raid" section, which describes thirteen sites associated with the Raid that have extant remains.

The *General* is the most revered and famous locomotive in the world. It was the star of the Civil War Great Locomotive Chase (a.k.a. Andrews Raid). It was the subject of at least three movies, including "Railroad Raiders of '62", "The General", starring Buster Keaton, and "The Great Locomotive Chase" starring Fess Parker. It has been the subject of countless books and articles.

The later history of the General is almost as exciting as the Chase itself. In April 1962, the *General* retraced its route from the Great Locomotive Chase under its own power. From 1967-1970, the *General* was the center of a complicated legal battle between Chattanooga, Tennessee (on one side) and the L&N Railroad and the State of Georgia (on the other side). Part of this battle included the blockading of the main line of the old W&A railroad just south of Chattanooga, TN. The legal battle went all the way to the U.S. Supreme Court to be resolved.

In the "Retracing the Route of the Andrews Raid" section, I rely heavily on William Pittenger's accounts of the Raid. While it is fashionable in some quarters today to criticize Pittenger's accounts (well, he *does* tend to make himself the hero of the Raid in many places), it remains the best first hand account of the Raid, with the original version being written in 1862/1863.

Some might question the amount of material in this book on Big Shanty (Kennesaw), This is partially because, as President of the Kennesaw Historical Society, I have access to a lot of Big Shanty material. However, as Big Shanty was the starting point of the Raid, and the eventual home of the *General*, I don't feel I need to provide too much apology for its prominence in this book.

I hope you enjoy this brief history of *The W&A, the General, and the Andrews Raid*.

- Robert Jones, August 2010

The Coming of the Western & Atlantic Railroad

On **December 21, 1836**, the Western and Atlantic Railroad was born. The Georgia legislature authorized the building of a state-owned railroad from Chattanooga to Terminus, Georgia (now Atlanta). Companion legislation was passed by the Tennessee General Assembly on **January 24, 1838**, which allowed the railroad to be constructed into Tennessee.

In **1837**, a survey for the nascent Western & Atlantic Railroad was conducted by S.H. Long, Chief Engineer of the Western and Atlantic railroad. The survey was presented on December 29, 1837 "To his excellency George R. Gilmer - Governor of Georgia, Milledgeville, Ga." Some excerpts follow.

> Sir: I embrace the earliest opportunity to forward my report on the surveys executed under my direction, with a view to the selection of the most favorable route for a railroad from the Chattahoochee river to the Tennessee line... (57-2, 57-3)

> The difficult and arduous task of discovering and choosing the most favorable route for a railroad, leading from a point in the Tennessee line, "at or near Rossville," to some point on the Chattahoochee between Winn's Ferry and Campbellton, separated from each other by a distance of seventy miles, has, by law, devolved upon me, as Chief Engineer of the Western and Atlantic railroad of the State of Georgia. Deeply impressed with the high responsibilities thus imposed, I embarked, as early as practicable, in a careful and thorough examination of the country, with a view to the effectual discharge of the duties of my appointment. (57-3)

> **The country alluded to constitutes a very respectable portion of the region at present occupied by the Cherokee Indians, and generally designated as Cherokee country.** It embraces that part of Georgia situated between the Chattahoochee river and the State of Tennessee. Its extent on the Chattahoochee, from Winn's Ferry to Campbellton, is about 70 miles, and on the Tennessee line, about half that distance, from Rossville eastwards; while its

length, from north to south, is about 100 miles. **Within this district are comprised the counties of Walker, Murray, Floyd, Cass, Cherokee, Forsyth, Paulding, Cobb, and a part of Campbell, all of which, except Paulding and Campbell, have county seats within the district.** Its population is, as yet, very sparse, compared with the amount that might find most ample and comfortable subsistence therein; a very inconsiderable proportion of its surface is yet cleared and under cultivation... (57-4)

That portion of the district situated between the Chattahoochee river and the Blue ridge, **constitutes a part of the gold district of Georgia,** and contains several of the most productive gold mines of the State. The mines near Scudder's, Allatoona, and Burnt Hickory, are of this character. (57-5)

With respect to the general elevation of the ridge dividing between the waters of the Chattahoochee and Etowah, which becomes coincident with the main spur of the Blue Ridge, near the Kinnesaw, Pine, and other mountains, at the sources of Allatoona, Pumpkinvine, Raccoon, Uharley, and Sweetwater creeks: This elevation...evidently decreases as we proceed northeastwardly from the sources of the Tallapoosa river, Sweetwater, and Uharley creeks, towards the center of Forsyth county... (57-5)

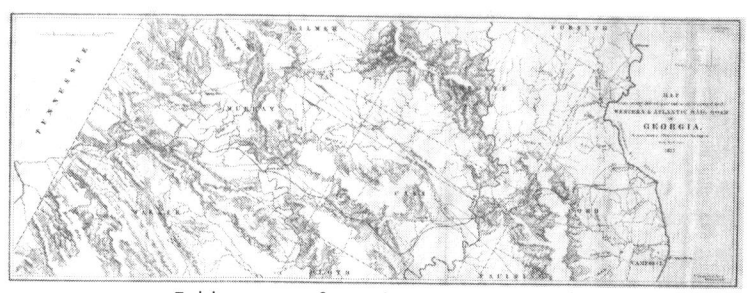

Fold-out map from the original survey[1]

Commencing on the Chattahoochee near Montgomery's ferry, **the road crosses the Chattahoochee, and ascends to Marietta, the seat of justice for Cobb county.** It there crosses the Kennesaw summit, on the north side of the mountain of the same name, and **descends towards the Etowah, passing through the village of Allatoona.**

---
[1] Library of Congress G3921.P3 1837 .C6 RR 613

The 2d section, passing through the village of Marietta, is eight and half miles in length, and terminates at the point where the Kennesaw mountain intersects the ridge upon which its whole distance is coursed. By examining the profile, this will be found to be the most elevated summit between the Chattahoochee and Etowah rivers, 437 feet above the former, and 482 feet above the latter.

The cost of a railroad, graded for two tracks, and furnished with one track only, has been computed only for the shortest of the routes above mentioned, viz: for the route extending from the Chattahoochee to the Red Clay council ground. Agreeably to the computation, the aggregate cost of road formulation, inclusive of bridges, culverts &c., is $1,095,597 50, or $10,142 28 per mile; and the aggregate cost of the road complete, with a single track, is $1,851,756 59, or $17,142 28 per mile. To this cost should be added fifteen per cent, to cover contingencies, engineering, superintendence &c., which will be for the aggregate cost of $2,129,920 08, or $19,713 62 per mile; a very small expenditure, compared with the cost of other similar works in the United States.

Whenever the exigencies of trade and transportation shall require the addition of a second track, which will no doubt prove to be the case within the period of a very few years from the first opening of the road, the cost for the additional track may be assumed at $6,000 per mile.

The Western and Atlantic railroad, when viewed in its relations to the natural and artificial channels of trade and intercourse above considered, is to be regarded as the main connecting link of a chain or system of internal improvements, more splendid and imposing than any other that has ever been devised in this or any other country. In contemplating the widely extended and incalculable benefits, in a civil or military, moral or commercial, and even religious point of view, that must undoubtedly result from its consummation, **we are overwhelmed with the flood of magnificent results that breaks upon us.** Among these, we venture to advert to one of the innumerable advantages hereafter to result from the sources above contemplated, in relation to which the south is most deeply interested, viz: the repopulation and reclamation of the worn out and deserted fields every where to be met with, in other parts of all the Southern States, by industrious white inhabitants, who will "replenish the waste places", and restore fertility to the exhausted glebe. With such an enterprise, and the means of its accomplishment in hand, and with such prospects inviting to its vigorous prosecution in view what destinies are too might, and what magnificence too exalted, for the anticipations of Georgia?[2]

Engineering obstacles

The W&A wasn't completely finished until **1850**. While some of the delay can be ascribed to inefficiency, the W&A was also a great engineering challenge for its time. The W&A was very crooked, with 10,000 degrees of curvatures in 138 miles – enough to make 28 complete circles! Superintendent John W. Lewis stated in his 1860 annual report that the W&A was "the crookedest road under the sun". Along with having to cross several rivers, including the Chattahoochee, the Etowah, and the Oostanaula, the W&A also had to tunnel through the Chetoogeta Mountain (Tunnel Hill) at the northern end of the line.

Construction

By **1838**, over 500 men (including some Cherokee Indians) were at work on grading, road bed, and trestles. In **1840**, the original engineer on the project, S. H. Long, tendered his resignation after being criticized for slow progress. He would not be the last W&A engineer to resign for that reason.

In **1842**, Charles Garnett was appointed the new chief engineer. More auspiciously, a wooden office was built in Terminus, cementing Atlanta as the future base of operations of the W&A railroad.

By **1845**, the first 20 miles of track were in operation, allowing goods and passengers to travel from Terminus to the County Seat of Cobb County, Marietta.

---

[2] 1837 W&A Survey, S.H. Long (Courtesy Southern Museum of Civil War and Locomotive History)

Marietta Square, 1864[3]

As the railroad was constructed north, small towns grew up along the right of way, including Vinings, Smyrna and Big Shanty (Kennesaw). The latter was so named because of the collection of railroad shanties built there to house railroad workers and equipment. There were still 19th railroad shanties in Kennesaw in the 1990s. The the last two were torn down in **1994**.

The last railroad shanties in Big Shanty (Kennesaw), in 1994

One of the most significant engineering obstacles on the W&A was located several miles north of Big Shanty – Allatoona Pass. The cut is (mostly) through solid rock, and is about 360 feet long, and 180 feet deep. A small town grew up here - Allatoona Pass in the Fall of 1864 had eight homes, some small stores, a railroad depot, and

---
[3] Library of Congress http://www.loc.gov/pictures/item/92501326

Union supply warehouses. A great Civil War battle was fought there on **October 5, 1864** (Union victory).

By 1847, the W&A was completed to Dalton, and Chief Engineer Garnett resigned. In 1848, he was replaced by William L. Mitchell as Chief Engineer.

This early 20th century photo shows Nellie and Helen Garrett posing in front of a W&A railroad "shanty" or section house. Nellie and Helen were daughters of Henry C. Garrett, an NC&StL Railroad section foreman. (From the collection of Helen Odom)

In **1849,** the greatest engineering obstacle on the route, Tunnel Hill, was completed.

Civil War drawing of Tunnel Hill. A photo of the tunnel as it appears today can be found in the "Retracing the Route of the Andrews Raid" chapter.[4]

On **May 9, 1850**, the first train traveled over the entire length of the W&A! The final cost of the railroad to the State of Georgia was $4,087,925.

---

[4] Library of Congress LC-USZC4-5682

This April 1851 W&A schedule shows the stops between Atlanta and Chattanooga[5]

Organization

By May 1850, the W&A was up and running, hauling passengers and freight between Atlanta and Chattanooga. In charge of the railroad was a Superintendent, who reported to the Governor of Georgia (remember, it was a State-owned and operated railroad at this point). Other key positions included:

- Treasurer
- Master of Transportation – in charge of the daily operation of trains, stations and track
- Master Machinist – in charge of shops, locomotive and rolling stock maintenance. The shops were located in Atlanta.

[5] From *American Railways Guide for the United States* (Curran Dinsmore, April 1851)

Facts and figures

The W&A started out as 5-foot gauge. Most of its early locomotives were of the 4-4-0 "American" style, made famous by the General.

- All of the locomotives in the 1850s were wood burners
- It took 3.5 cords of wood to go from Atlanta to Chattanooga
- A typical train was 6-20 cars
- The average speed was 10 miles per hour
- A train crew was comprised of an engineer, fireman and wood-passer

Enter the General and the Texas

In **1855**, The *General,* the most famous locomotive in W&A history (perhaps in all American railroading history), was completed in December, built by Rogers, Ketchum & Grosvenor of Paterson, NJ. It cost $8,850. In January 1856, the *General* went into service hauling freight on the W&A. The second most famous locomotive from the Great Locomotive Chase was the Texas, which was built in **1856** by Danforth, Cooke & Company, and put into service by the W&A in October.

The General was built as a classic 4-4-0 American wood burner, with a balloon stack (Radley and Hunter type). Some of the specs of the *General* as built include:

- There was no brake on engine (although there was a brake on the tender). In those days, an engine was braked by putting it into reverse.
- Original Gauge: 5 ft (this would change in 1886)
- Driver wheels diameter: 60"
- Total weight: 50,300 lbs.
- Capacity of tender: 1.75 cords of wood

Civil War Years – 1861-1862

W&A roundhouse (background) in Atlanta, GA[6]

The Civil War was very profitable for the W&A – at least until Sherman arrived in Georgia. In **1861, t**he Net earnings of the W&A were $541,041. This rose to $998,270 the following year.

In **October 1861**, Governor Joseph E. Brown threatened military force against the Confederate government if locomotives or rolling stock were seized for the War effort. This is a reminder that many of the Georgians that fought on the side of the Confederacy did so under the auspices of the Georgia Militia, and not the Confederate army.

---

[6] LOC http://www.loc.gov/pictures/item/cwp2003005466/PP

In **1862**, the W&A had 46 locomotives in service, with 10 in need of repair. The W&A started to be impacted by the War, as two W&A bridges across the Chickamauga were burned by Union forces. A new innovation in warfare started to be used by both North and South – transporting troops by railroad. The first large troop movements involving the W&A occurred in **1862**. A head-on collision in **July 1862** killed 12 and injured 36.

W&A water tower (Civil War era)[7]

The condition of the physical infrastructure of the W&A during the Civil War could be described as precarious. William Pittenger, a member of Andrews Raiders, described the condition of the W&A in April of 1862:

> We found the railroad, however, to be of the roughest and most difficult character. The grades were very heavy and the curves numerous and sharp. We seemed to be running towards every point of the compass. The deep valleys and steep hills of this part of the country had rendered the building of the road difficult and costly. There were numerous high embankments where an accident would be of deadly character. The track was also uneven and in generally bad condition, for the war had rendered railroad

---

[7] Library of Congress http://www.loc.gov/pictures/item/2004660538

iron scarce and high-priced, besides diverting all attention and resources into other channels.[8]

On **April 12, 1862**, the most famous event in the history of the W&A occurred - The Great Locomotive Chase, also known as Andrews Raid. On that day, 20 Union Spies, led by civilian James J. Andrews seized a Confederate locomotive named the *General* at Big Shanty, Georgia (now Kennesaw). The train was stopped for a 20-minute breakfast break at the Lacy Hotel.

---
[8] *Capturing a Locomotive* by William Pittenger (National Tribune, 1881)

The Great Locomotive Chase

"Pulling out of Big Shanty"[9]

The Andrews Raid was part of a bigger strategy on the part of Union Major General Ormsby Mitchel. Mitchel was in charge of defending Nashville, and he soon set he sights on Huntsville, Alabama and Chattanooga, Tennessee. Working with a civilian spy, James J. Andrews, a plan was formulated whereby Andrews would lead a group of raiders deep into the heart of the Confederacy in Georgia to steal a train north of Atlanta and steam north to Chattanooga. The goal – to destroy as much of the railroad and communications infrastructure between Atlanta and Chattanooga as possible, thus cutting Chattanooga off from assistance from Atlanta during the planned Union attach there.

---

[9] *Capturing a Locomotive* by William Pittenger (National Tribune, 1881)

"Portrait of Brig. Gen. Ormsby M. Mitchel, officer of the Federal Army"[10]

The plan was probably sound, however, the devil is in the execution. Most of the raiding party arrived a day late to the embarkation point for the raid, Marietta, GA. Thus, Andrews and his raiders were a day behind schedule. When the raid commenced on April 12, 1862, they were dogged by trains coming southbound from Chattanooga to Atlanta (as the Union offensive was already in full motion). Also, heavy rains made it impossible to burn the several wooden bridges along the W&A route between Atlanta and Chattanooga.

Andrews, a civilian, is a bit of a mystery. Andrews was a native of Hancock County, now West Virginia. He appears to have been a smuggler running contraband between the lines. How he, as a

---

[10] Library of Congress
http://www.loc.gov/pictures/item/cwp2003000359/PP

civilian, ended up leading a military expedition behind enemy lines is not altogether clear.

William Pittenger, one of the Raiders, later described Andrews in this way:

> Mr. Andrews was nearly six feet in height, or powerful frame, black hair, and long, black, and silken beard, Roman features, a high and expansive forehead, and a voice fine and soft as a woman's. Of polished manners, stately presence, and more than ordinary personal beauty, wide information, great shrewdness and sagacity, he was admirably fitted to win favor in a community like that of the South, which has always placed a high value on personal qualities. He had also the clear forethought in devising complicated schemes, and the calmness in the hour of danger necessary for the perilous game he played.[11]

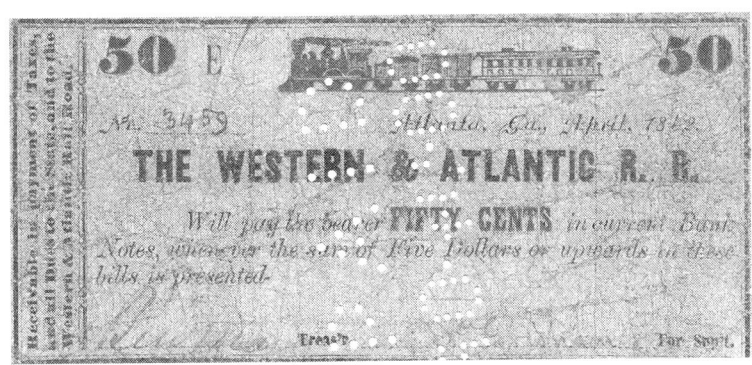

W&A script – dated April 1862

The *General* had arrived in Big Shanty at about 6:00 a.m. Most of the passengers (and all of the crew) left the train and headed to the Lacy Hotel. It was at this moment that Andrews and his raiders struck. After uncoupling the passenger cars from the rest of the train, the three raider locomotive engineers and Andrews jumped in the cab, while the rest of the 16 raiders piled into the boxcars still coupled to the train. The *General* headed north, under the hand of Engineer William J. Knight. Within seconds, the train crew began the chase on foot.

---

[11] *Capturing a Locomotive* by William Pittenger (National Tribune, 1881)

The raid entered into legend because the conductor of the train, William A. Fuller, and Western & Atlantic Railroad Superintendent of Motive Power Anthony Murphy pursued the stolen train for 87 miles, by foot, hand car, and three different locomotives, until the train was finally abandoned two miles north of Ringgold, Georgia.

Aftermath

All of the raiders were captured, with the following results:

- 8 were hung, including James J. Andrews
- 8 escaped, and made it back to Union lines
- 6 were involved in a prisoner exchange

Twenty of the 22 original military members of the raid received the Congressional Medal of Honor. As a civilian, Andrews did not receive the award.

The Great Locomotive Chase has been commemorated in numerous books, and at least two major Hollywood movies, including the **1926** *The General*, starring Buster Keaton, and the **1956** Walt Disney movie *The Great Locomotive Chase* starring Fess Parker. The first film on the raid was produced in 1911 by Kalem, a short silent movie named *Railroad Raiders of '62*.

In **1972**, the *General* went on permanent display in the Kennesaw Civil War Museum (now the Southern Museum of Civil War and Locomotive History). The third of the pursuing locomotives, the *Texas*, is enshrined at the Atlanta Cyclorama.

After the raid, minor repairs were made on the *General* in Ringgold, GA. On **May 2, 1862**, the *General* was used to transport raiders from Swims Jail in Chattanooga to Atlanta.

"Buster Keaton in 'The General'"[12]

The next chapter tells the history of the raid, and shows what is left to see at the sites today.

---

[12] Library of Congress http://www.loc.gov/pictures/item/ggb2006005343

Retracing the Route of the Andrews Raid

Stop #1 – The Kennesaw House

At midnight, we were wakened by the conductor calling "Marietta." The goal was reached. We were in the center of the Confederacy, with our deadly enemies all around. Before we left, we were to strike a blow that would either make all rebeldom vibrate to the center, or be ourselves at the mercy of the merciless. It was a time for solemn thought; but we were too weary to indulge in speculations of the future.[13]

Significance to the raid:

The raiders spent the night prior to the raid at the Fletcher House (now Kennesaw House), in Marietta, GA. They boarded the northbound train pulled by the General at about 5:00am, on April 12, 1862.

The Kennesaw House in Marietta, GA

---

[13] *Daring and Suffering: A History of the Andrews Railroad Raid* by William Pittenger (J. W. Daughaday, 1863)

What is left to see:

The Kennesaw House is still intact, and is now the home of the Marietta Museum of History. Also check out the famous Marietta Square, and the rebuilt Marietta Depot.

How to get there:

The Kennesaw House is located one block west of the Marietta Square, by the CSX tracks.

STOP #2 - Kennesaw, Georgia

When our train pulled up to the platform the usual announcement was shouted, "Big Shanty; twenty minutes for breakfast!" Most fortunately for us, the conductor, engineer, firemen, and train-hands generally, with many of the passengers, poured out, and hurried to the long, low eating-room which gave its name to the station. The engine was utterly unguarded...Andrews went forward to examine the track and see if there was any hindrance to a rapid rush ahead. Almost immediately he returned, and said, very quietly, "All right, boys, let us go now."...We rose, left the cars, and walked briskly to the head of the train. With the precision of machinery, every man took his appointed place. Three cars back from the tender the coupling-pin was drawn out, as the load of passenger-cars would only have been an incumbrance. Wilson W. Brown, who acted as engineer, William Knight as assistant, Alfred Wilson as fireman, together with Andrews, mounted the engine, Knight grasping the lever, and waiting the word for starting...At a signal from Andrews, the remainder of the band, who had kept watch, climbed with surprising quickness into a boxcar which stood open. All was well! Knight, at Andrews' orders, jerked open the steam-valve, and we were off! Before the camp-guards or the bystanders could do more than turn a curious eye upon our proceedings, the train was under way, and we were safe from interruption.[14]

Significance to the raid:

On April 12, 1862, at approximately 6:00 AM, the Confederate locomotive *General*, hauling a passenger train from Atlanta to Chattanooga, made a scheduled 20 minute stop at the four-room Lacy Hotel, in the town of Big Shanty, Georgia (now Kennesaw, GA). At 6:10 AM, James Andrews and 20 Union spies seized the engine, and three cars, and began their fateful trip north.

What is left to see:

The Lacy Hotel was burned to the ground by William Tecumseh Sherman's troops in 1864, after the fall of Atlanta. The location of

---

[14] *Capturing a Locomotive* by William Pittenger (National Tribune, 1881)

the hotel foundation is (probably) under the current Depot parking lot. The most significant remains from the raid is the *General* itself, located in the Southern Museum of Civil War and Locomotive History, on Cherokee street in Kennesaw. Also, there is a stone marker commemorating the Raid in the little park at the corner of Cherokee St. and Rt. 293, as well as a monument to William Fuller.

Southern Museum of Civil War & Locomotive History

How to get there:

Take exit 273, Wade Green Road, from I-75. Head west (Cherokee St.) approx. 2.3 miles. The museum is on your right, before the railroad crossing (the old Western & Atlantic line!)

Monument to William Fuller, located in the little park at the corner of Cherokee St. and Rt. 293

STOP #3 - Moon's Station

> They put on all their speed, and ran along the track for three miles, when they came across some track-raisers, who had a small truck-car, which is shoved along by men so employed on railroads, on which to carry their tools. This truck and men were at once "impressed." They took it by turns of two at a time to run behind this truck, and push it along all up grades and level portions of the road, and let it drive at will on all the down grades.[15]

Significance to the raid:

This desolate little spot, located about 2 miles north along the old W&A railroad right of way, was the site where Andrews stopped momentarily to "borrow" some tools from an obliging railroad crew. These tools included a crowbar later used to tear up track!

This is also where Fuller and Murphy picked up the now famous "pole car" or "truck-car" used to pursue the raiders all the way to the Etowah River.

What is left to see:

A State of Georgia marker is the only thing left to commemorate the part of Moon's Station in the raid. The railroad crossing was closed in 1995.

---

[15] *Southern Confederacy*, April 15, 1862, Atlanta, GA

Moon's Station

How to get there:

From the museum, head back toward I-75 (Cherokee Street). Travel 2 miles, and turn left at Baker Road. Travel .7 miles, and turn right to continue on Baker Road. Moon's Station is .3 miles on the left. (Note: Moon's Station Rd. no longer crosses the railroad tracks at Moon's Station).

STOP #4 - Etowah River Bridge

Extensive iron-furnaces were located on the Etowah River, about five miles above the station. These works were connected with the railroad by a private track, which was the property of Major Cooper, as well as he works themselves. Murphy knew that Major Cooper had also bought an engine called the "Yonah." It had been built in the shop over which Murphy presided, and was one of the best locomotives in the State...

...Fuller, Murphy, and Cain, with the several armed men they had picked up at the stations passed, could not repress shouts of exultation when they saw the old "Yonah" standing on the main track, ready fired up, and headed towards Kingston. It had just arrived from the mines, and in a short time would have returned again. Thus a new element of tremendous importance, which had been ignored in all our calculations, was introduced into the contest.

The pursuers seized their inestimable prize, called for all the volunteers who could snatch guns at a moment's notice, and were soon swiftly but cautiously rushing with the power of steam towards Kingston.[16]

Significance to the raid:

This bridge was the first main target of Andrews' master plan. Andrews made a decision not to destroy the bridge, as the Cooper Iron Works locomotive *Yonah* was in sight on a nearby spur track. The decision not to destroy the bridge (and the *Yonah*) proved to be fatal, as the *Yonah* was the first locomotive used by Fuller and Murphy in the chase.

What is left to see:

The massive stone bridge supports are easily viewable from Highway 41, south of Cartersville. The bridge itself was destroyed in 1864 during Sherman's Atlanta campaign.

---

[16] *Capturing a Locomotive* by William Pittenger (National Tribune, 1881)

Remains of the old Etowah Railroad bridge (Photo by Lynda Bricker)

How to get there:

Continue north on Baker Rd for 1.1 miles. Turn left on Hickory Grove Rd. (turns into Southside Dr. in Acworth). Travel 3 miles into Acworth, GA, and turn left across the railroad tracks on Lemon St. (you'll pass the ruins of an old mill (now a restaurant) on the left before Lemon St.) Turn right onto Main St. (SR293). Continue north on SR293 (approx. 6.4 miles) to the intersection of SR293 and US41. Turn left to go under US41. Continue north on SR293 through Emerson, GA for approximately 2.4 miles. Turn right on River Road. Cross under Route 41 (.4 miles). Immediately on the right are the remains of the Civil War era Etowah River Bridge.

Alternate route bypassing Acworth and Emerson: From Moon's Station, return to I-75. Take I-75 to exit 283. Turn left (west) on Old Allatoona Road[17]. Turn right (north) at US 41. The bridge piers are about 3.5 miles north on US41, as you cross the Etowah River.

---

[17] If you turn right instead of left, you can see Allatoona Pass (2.1 miles)

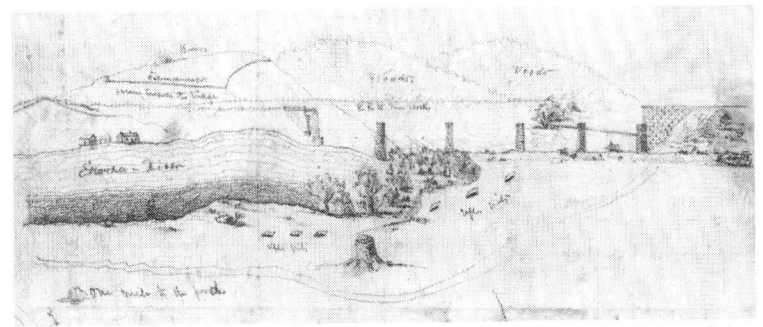

This 1864 drawing shows a "View of fortifications near the ruins of the Western and Atlantic Railroad bridge across the Etowah River in Georgia"[18]

---

[18] Library of Congress http://hdl.loc.gov/loc.gmd/g3923b.cws00080

STOP #5 - Cooper Furnace

Significance to the raid:
The *Yonah*, the first locomotive used to pursue Andrews and his raiders, was in use at Cooper Furnace, located on the banks of the Etowah River. The iron works were operated by Major Mark Cooper from 1847 - 1862, hence the name it still bears today.

What is left to see:
The huge iron foundry still stands, as well as traces of the old railroad cut on the north side of the River Road.

Cooper Furnace

How to get there:
From the Etowah River bridge piers, continue east on the River Road (about 2.4 miles) until you dead-end at Cooper Furnace.

STOP #6 - Cass Station

We thus continued - running a little ahead of time, then stopping to obstruct the track and cut the wire - until Cass Station was reached, where we took on a good supply of wood and water. At this place we also obtained a complete time schedule of the road. Andrews told the tank-tender that we were running a powder-train through to the army of General Beauregard at Corinth, which was almost out of ammunition, and that the greatest haste was necessary. He further claimed to be a Confederate officer of high. rank, and said that he had impressed this train for the purpose in hand, and that Fuller, with the regular passenger train, would be along shortly. The whole story was none too plausible, as General Mitchel was now interposed between our present position and Beauregard, and we would never have been able to get a train to the army of the latter on this route; but the tender was not critical and gave us his schedule, adding that he would willingly sell his shirt to Beauregard if that general needed it. When this man was afterwards asked if he did not suspect the character of the enemy he thus aided, he answered that he would as soon have suspected the President of the Confederacy himself as one who talked so coolly and confidently as Andrews did![19]

Significance to the raid:

The Raiders stopped for wood & water at Cass Station. The over-eager tender, William Russell, gave Andrews a W&A schedule, thinking that he was helping the Confederate War effort! (Andrews had told Russell that the General was taking much needed ammunition to General Beauregard).

---

[19] *Capturing a Locomotive* by William Pittenger (National Tribune, 1881)

Site of Cass Station

What is left to see:

Scant remains behind the brick warehouse may be of a warehouse that stood at the time of the Raid.

How to get there:

From Cooper's Furnace, head west on the River Road, back to US41. Take US41 north through Cartersville for 7 miles. Turn left on Mac Johnson Rd. Turn right on SR293. Turn left on Burnt Hickory Rd. Cass Station is about 200 yards on the right.

STOP #7 – Kingston

> One precious hour had we wasted at Kingston, - time enough to have burned every bridge between that place and Dalton! The whole margin of time on which we had allowed ourselves to count was two hours; now half of that was thrown away at one station, and nothing accomplished. We dared wait no longer. Andrews decided to rush ahead with the intention of meeting this extra train wherever it might be found; and forcing it to back before him to the next siding, where he could pass it. The resolution was in every way dangerous, but the danger would at least be of an active character. Just at this moment the long-expected whistle was heard, and soon the train came into plain view, bringing with it an almost interminable string of cars. The weight and length of its train had caused the long delay. Obedient to direction, it followed the first extra down the main track, and its locomotive was a long way removed from the depot when the last car cleared the upper end of the side track on which we lay. At length it had got far enough down, and it was possible for us to push on.[20]

Significance to the raid:

Andrews was delayed here for 65 minutes, because of a three-section southbound freight. Fuller arrived a mere 4 minutes after Andrews pulled out of Kingston! (Fuller later claimed that he made the 14 mile trip from the Etowah River to Kingston in the *Yonah* in 15 minutes!) The *Yonah* was abandoned, and Fuller and Murphy navigated the complicated Kingston rail yard on foot. The Rome Railroad locomotive *William R. Smith* was appropriated next, by Fuller and Murphy.

What is left to see:

A State of Georgia marker commemorating the raid; foundations of the old railroad station; the roadbed of the old railroad spur to Rome, GA is visible in places. The cool DeSoto Hotel was built in 1890.

---

[20] *Capturing a Locomotive* by William Pittenger (National Tribune, 1881)

Rome Railroad connection to the W&A

How to get there:

From Cass Station, return to SR293. Turn left, and follow SR293 towards Kingston, about 6.5 miles. Turn left at the blinking light onto Shaw Ave, and follow the road to the center of Kingston. The remains of the station are across the railroad tracks from the DeSoto Hotel. The remains of the Rome railroad spur are to the west of the station remains, in what is now a public park.

STOP #8 – Adairsville

A short distance south of Adairsville we again stopped, and Andrews called us to come forth and work with a will. No exhortation was needed. John Scott, as usual, climbed the telegraph-pole; and the wire was soon severed. Two or three rails were slowly and painfully battered loose with our iron bar, which still constituted our only instrument for track-lifting. These were loaded on the car to carry away with us...

We reached Adairsville before the expected freight, but had only just taken our place on the sidetrack when its whistle was heard. When it came up, Andrews, who still personated a Confederate officer, and exacted and received the obedience which in those days of conscription and impressment was readily yielded to military authority, ordered the train to be run past the station and back again on the side track behind his own, to wait for the expected passenger train. The usual explanations about the powder train were repeated to credulous ears. Then came five minutes of suspense and waiting. The train was behind time, - a trifling matter in itself, but, in our situation, each minute might turn the scale between death and life. We could not afford 'to repeat the experience of Kingston. Not one bridge had yet been burned, and all we could show for our hazard, beside our captured train, were a few cross-ties and lifted rails.[21]

Significance to the raid:
Andrews was once again delayed at the Adairsville station. Just south of Adairsville, Fuller was forced to abandoned the *William R. Smith*, and continue pursuit in the famous *Texas*.

What is left to see:
The 1847 railroad station contains a small museum dedicated to the Chase; a marble monument that mentions the chase.

---
[21] *Capturing a Locomotive* by William Pittenger (National Tribune, 1881)

1847 Adairsville Depot (now a museum)

Stone marker next to the Adairsville Depot

How to get there:

From Kingston, return to SR293 on Shaw St. Turn left on SR293, and travel .4 miles. Turn right on Halls Station Road, and follow the old

W&A railroad tracks to Adairsville (approx. 9.5 miles). Turn right on King St. Turn right on Railroad St. (not marked), and continue to the old depot.

Stop #9 – Calhoun

At Calhoun, Fuller scarcely made a full stop. He told his tale in a few words and called for volunteers. A number came just as he was moving on again; indeed, after the train was well under way, he secured a still more valuable prize. The telegraph managers at Chattanooga had found that the wires were broken, and were endeavoring to discover the source of mischief. By telegraphing to different stations and asking for replies, they could easily make an approximate estimate. But the difficulty was coming nearer: they discovered that one station after another was being cut off from communication with headquarters. South of Calhoun they could get no reply at the time the passenger train reached Dalton. They had, therefore, directed the only operator at that station - a mere boy - to leave his post and go to Calhoun for the purpose of discovering and remedying the mischief. Fuller recognized him on the platform, and reached out his hand, shouting, "Come!" The boy took hold and was lifted on the flying engine.[22]

Significance to the raid:

Fuller picked up Dalton telegrapher Edward Henderson, who had come south to see why the telegraph lines were down. Henderson would (successfully) send a telegraph to Chattanooga from Dalton. Also, the Raiders cut telegraph wire and released the 1st box car between Calhoun and Resaca (the Oostanaula River).

What is left to see:

The 1847 depot at Calhoun is still standing, and is now owned by the City of Calhoun.

How to get there:

From Adairsville, head north on Main Street (Old 41) to SR 140, turn right (east) on SR 140, to I-75. Head north on I-75 to exit 312. At exit 312 head west on SR 53, bearing to the right as you reach US41. The Calhoun depot is at the intersection of Court and King Streets. As you continue on US41 into downtown Calhoun, turn left on Court Street, and you'll see the depot on the left.

---

[22] *Capturing a Locomotive* by William Pittenger (National Tribune, 1881)

1847 Calhoun depot

STOP #10 - Oostanuala River Bridge (Resaca)

Now the Oostenaula [sic] bridge was in sight, and we slackened speed for a desperate attempt to burn it. But before we could come to a full stop the pursuer was close upon us, and very reluctantly we steamed over the bridge and continued our flight.[23]

Significance to the raid:

The Oostanuala River Bridge was one of the primary targets for destruction by Andrews Raiders. The wet, soggy conditions kept the wooden covered bridge from catching fire.

What is left to see:

The stone ramparts of the modern railroad bridge date from the time of the Raid.

How to get there:

From Calhoun, continue north on US41. From the point where you intersect with I-75, head north on US41 for 1.4 miles. The stone ramparts of the old railroad bridge are on the right.

---

[23] *Capturing a Locomotive* by William Pittenger (National Tribune, 1881)

Stop #11 – Dalton Depot

Significance to the raid:
The *Texas*, now in close pursuit of the *General*, stopped briefly at the 1847 Dalton depot to drop off telegrapher Edward Henderson. Henderson had traveled south to Calhoun to see why he couldn't receive telegraphs from the south. From Dalton, Henderson telegraphed to Chattanooga:

> To General Leadbetter, Commander at Chattanooga
>
> My train was captured this A.M. At Big Shanty, evidently by Federal soldiers in disguise. They are making rapidly for Chattanooga, possibly with the idea of burning the railroad bridges in their rear. If I do not capture them in the mean time see that they do not pass Chattanooga.
>
> William A. Fuller[24]

Two miles north of Dalton, the raiders blocked the tracks and cut the telegraph wires, but the message had already been sent.

What is left to see:
The depot at Dalton is still standing, and now operates as a restaurant and tavern ("The Dalton Depot").

How to get there:
From the Oostanaula River Bridge in Resaca, travel north on US41 200 yards. Turn left on SR136. Travel about .3 miles, and get on I-75 North. Head north on I-75 to exit 333. Head east on SR52 (W. Walnut Ave.) about 1.8 miles. Turn left (north) on S. Thornton Ave. After about .72 miles, turn right (east) on W. Crawford St., which dead-ends into Depot Street. The Depot is located at 110 Depot St.

---

[24] *Capturing a Locomotive* by William Pittenger (National Tribune, 1881)

The 1852 "Dalton Depot"

STOP #12 - Tunnel Hill

..they shot on, and passed through the great tunnel at Tunnel Hill, being there only five minutes behind. The fugitives, thus finding themselves closely pursued, uncoupled two of the box-cars from the engine, to impede the progress of the pursuers. Fuller hastily coupled them to the front of his engine, and pushed them ahead of him, to the first turn-out or siding...[25]

Significance to the raid:

A major target of the Andrews Raid was the 1849 tunnel at Tunnel Hill. Andrews failed to destroy the tunnel, as the *Texas* was within site by that time.

What is left to see:

The stone building by the tracks is the original depot. The old tunnel is now part of a park, which includes a wonderful visitor center. Note: Use of the old tunnel was discontinued in 1928, when a new tunnel was built next to it.

Tunnel Hill Depot

---

[25] *Southern Confederacy*, April 15, 1862, Atlanta, GA

How to get there:

From the Dalton Depot, return to I-75. Head north on I-75 to exit 341 (SR201). Turn left (south) onto SR201. Travel for 2.5 miles, continuing straight on Varnell St, when SR201 turns to the right. Turn right on Main St. Turn left on Oak St., and cross the railroad tracks. Make a left on Clisby-Austin Rd. The visitor's center and the old depot is on the left. The tunnel mouth is ahead .3 miles on the left (after the covered bridge).

Entrance to the restored Tunnel Hill tunnel

STOP #13 – Ringgold

Thus the engine thieves passed Ringgold, where they began to fag. They were out of wood, water, and oil. Their rapid running and inattention to the engine had melted all the brass from the journals. They had no time to repair or refit, for an iron-horse of more bottom was close behind.[26]

Andrews and three others - Brown, Knight, and Alfred Wilson - were now on the engine, and the remaining sixteen were huddled together on the tender..."A few minutes before we came to the final halt, Andrews, Brown, Knight, and myself hastily discussed as to the best thing to be done, and it was concluded that the best course was to separate and scatter in all directions".

This fatal decision arose from two causes. Andrews, with all his courage, never rightly valued fighting men. He preferred accomplishing his objects by stratagem and in secrecy rather than by open force. It was simply wonderful that in all the exigencies of this expedition no one of his soldiers had been permitted to fire a single shot, or even to draw a revolver upon the enemy. He now considered that when scattered each one, as well as himself, would be able to find concealment, or if captured, to evade detection by false stories. This was a great mistake. The second reason for adopting this fatal course was the belief that the scattering of the party would also scatter pursuit, and make it less eager in any one direction. Under ordinary circumstances such would have been the result. But the terror and the fierce resentment aroused by the daring character of our enterprise caused the whole country to burst into a blaze of excitement, and the pursuit to be pushed with equal energy for scores of miles in every direction.[27]

---

[26] *Southern Confederacy*, April 15, 1862, Atlanta, GA
[27] *Capturing a Locomotive* by William Pittenger (National Tribune, 1881)

Significance to the raid:

The 1849 railroad depot was standing in Ringgold when Andrews Raiders, nearly out of wood and water for the *General*, limped past in 1862. The Great Chase ended 2 miles N. of the old depot, when the raiders abandoned the *General* and scattered into the woods.

What is left to see:

The old depot; a stone marker commemorating the end of the chase.

How to get there:

From the Tunnel Hill railroad tunnel, backtrack on Clisby-Austin road, and continue straight on Oak St to US41 (do not cross back over the railroad tracks). Head north on US41 for 7.1 miles, into Ringgold. The old depot will be on the hill to the right. From the depot, head north on SR151 (just S. of the depot - called Ootewah St./US41 Truck Route at the intersection below the depot) for 1.9 miles. The stone marker is on the left.

Marker located 2 miles north of Ringgold, indicating the end of the Chase

Other Spots to Visit

The *Texas*, the third of the pursuing locomotives, is located at the Atlanta Cyclorama, in Grant Park.

The *Texas*

There is a monument in Oakland Cemetery (located just north of Grant Park) to the seven Raiders who were hung nearby. There is a Georgia historical marker at Juniper and Third Streets that commemorates the spot where James J. Andrews was hung.

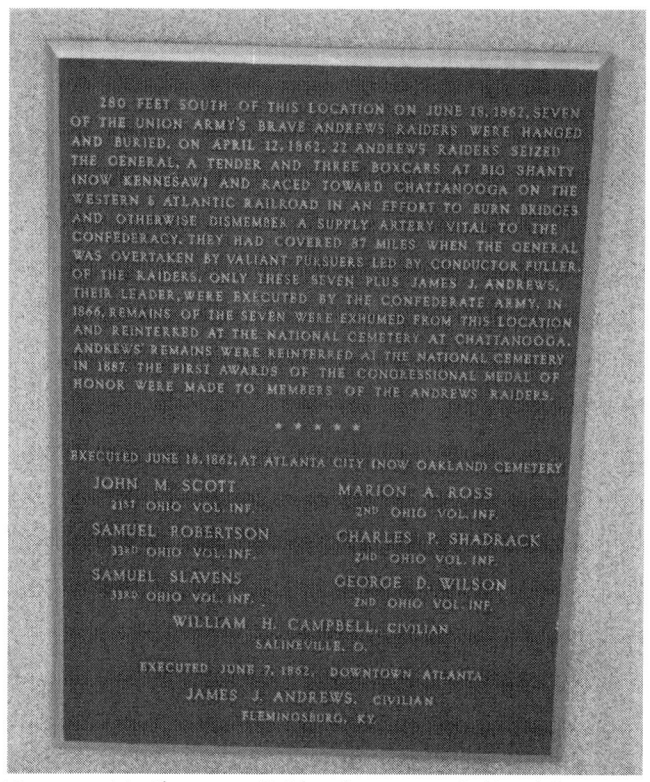

Monument to the seven Raiders hung near Oakland Cemetery

A nice monument to the raiders stands in the National Cemetery in Chattanooga, Tennessee.

c. 1902 photo showing the monument to the raiders in the National Cemetery, Chattanooga, TN[28]

While nothing much regarding the raid happened in Cartersville, GA, the wonderful 1856 depot that the *General* thundered by is still standing. Same thing with Allatoona Pass – well worth visiting, but nothing specific to the Raid happened there.

---

[28] LOC http://www.loc.gov/pictures/item/det1994006344/PP

Cartersville Depot

Entrance to Allatoona Pass. The tracks were torn up in the late 1940s when the railroad moved the right-of-way further away from Lake Allatoona. After the great flood in Atlanta in September 2009, the waters of Lake Allatoona were lapping up against the rim of the railroad cut north of the "deep cut", so I guess it was a smart idea to reroute the railroad in the 1940s.

Civil War – 1863-1865

W&A car shed. The name of the locomotive in the foreground is *Washington*.[29]

The Civil War continued to impact the W&A. In **1863**, Union cavalrymen (1700 in number) moved to disrupt the W&A east of Rome, but were defeated by Nathan Bedford Forrest. Employees of the W&A were organized into two military companies. Conductor William A. Fuller was put in charge of one of them, and commissioned as captain in the "Independent State Road Guards" by Governor Brown.

In **September 1863**, Longstreet's Corps was moved from Virginia to Georgia by train to fight in the Battle of Chickamauga. The last leg

---
[29] LOC http://www.loc.gov/pictures/item/cwp2003005462/PP

of the trip was on the W&A. Longstreet's Chief of Staff later commented on the condition of the southern railways in 1863:

> Never before were so many troops moved over such worn-out railways, none first-class from the beginning. Never were such crazy cars – passenger, baggage, mail, box, platform, all and any sort wobbling on the jumping strap-iron – used for hauling good soldiers. (Colonel G. Moxel Sorrell, Longstreet's Chief of Staff)

This was not the last time that the W&A would be used to bring troops to a battlefield in "a nick of time".

Railroad operations in Chattanooga after the Battle of Chickamauga[30]

In **May 1864**, William Tecumseh Sherman began his Atlanta campaign in Ringgold, GA. The W&A would have a key role in this famous Civil War campaign, serving as Sherman's vital supply line to the north right up until he began his March to the Sea in **mid-November 1864**. As Sherman moved south towards Atlanta, captured parts of the W&A were put under the administration of the US Military Railroads (USMRR).

---

[30] LOC http://www.loc.gov/pictures/item/cwp2003000855/PP

On **June 12, 1864**, Sherman issued an order that supply depots were to be built at Allatoona Pass, Acworth and Big Shanty on the W&A.

> During the temporary stay of the army at or near its present locality, the Army of the Tennessee will draw their supplies from the Big Shanty depot; the Army of the Cumberland from Acworth, and the Army of the Ohio from Allatoona.[31]

Acworth in 1864[32]

We get one very specific description of supplies that were dispersed from Big Shanty from Surgeon John Moore, U. S. Army, Medical Director – 2,500 pairs of underwear – no doubt well appreciated by the troops:

> Doctor Brewer arrived at Big Shanty with a large stock of everything in the way of supplies. These were at once issued to the surgeons in chief of division, who receipted for them and expended them in the division hospitals. Among these were 2,500 shirts and drawers.[33]

Big Shanty also served as a hospital for the Union Army. How this hospital made use of the W&A is described by Surgeon George E. Cooper, U. S. Army, Medical Director:

---

[31] *War of the Rebellion: Official Records of the Union and Confederate Armies*, U.S. Government Printing Office, 1891
[32] *Harper's Weekly* July 9, 1864
[33] *Op Cit*

A large field hospital, consisting of 100 tents, with all the appurtenances, had been organized, and was following in the rear of the army, at a convenient distance, keeping the line of the Western and Atlantic Railroad; into this the major portion of the wounded and sick were received and treated, until transportation to Chattanooga could be furnished them or their condition would permit of it...The wounded from the various assaults and skirmishers at and about Kenesaw [sic] were transferred from the division hospitals to Acworth and Big Shanty and thence by rail to Chattanooga.[34]

Big Shanty also served as Sherman's headquarters for the three weeks leading up to the Battle of Kennesaw Mountain. The great battle occurred on **June 27, 1864**, and the *General* was used as an ammunition train, and to transport wounded for General Johnston.

Big Shanty on June 10, 1864, showing the Union supply depot[35]

Although the Battle of Kennesaw Mountain was a defeat for Sherman's forces, Sherman eventually outflanked the Mountain, and continued towards Atlanta. On **July 9, 1864**, retreating Confederates forces destroyed a W&A bridge over the Chattahoochee River. On **August 5, 1864**, the USMRR ran the first train across the Chattahoochee under Union control.

---

[34] *Ibid*
[35] *Harper's Weekly*, July 9, 1864

c. 1891 painting of the Battle of Kennesaw Mountain[36]

On **September 2, 1864**, Atlanta fell to Sherman's army. The *General* was rendered inoperable by retreating Confederate troops. The USMRR began running trains into Atlanta on the W&A.

After the fall of Atlanta, the new headquarters of the W&A was established in Griswoldville, GA in **late-September 1864**. A mere two months later, Griswoldville was captured by Union forces during Sherman's March to the Sea. A famous battle occurred there on **November 22, 1864** when 3,700 Georgia Militia troops (comprised primarily of old men and boys) under General P.J. Phillips charged entrenched Union forces near Griswoldville across an open field. The Federals, who had Spencer repeating rifles, eventually drove the Militia off the field, inflicting heavy casualties (5:1, Confederate to Federals). The Union soldiers cared for the wounded Confederates through the night, and then left them for the locals to care for the next day.

All told, 28 locomotives and 391 cars were salvaged by the Confederacy from the Atlanta disaster.

---

[36] Library of Congress http://www.loc.gov/pictures/item/91482215

The *General* after the fall of Atlanta (Courtesy Southern Museum of Civil War and Locomotive History)

This 1864 George Barnard photo shows Union troops in the background on top of USMRR boxcars. In the foreground is an unidentified 4-4-0, and the office of the *Atlanta Intelligencer* newspaper, founded in 1849.[37]

During the **Fall of 1864**, the W&A was used as the primary supply line for Sherman's troops in Atlanta. Confederate General John Bell Hood briefly interrupted that supply line in **early October, 1864**, when Confederate troops succeeded in destroying 15 miles of track of the W&A from Big Shanty to Allatoona Pass. On **October 5, 1864** the Union again seized control of the W&A after the victory at the Battle of Allatoona Pass. Allatoona Pass was a Union victory partially because Union Brigadier General John Corse rushed men to the Union fortification at Allatoona Pass via the Rome and W&A Railroads the night before the battle.

Corse managed to ship 1,054 men from Rome to Allatoona Pass in

---

[37] LOC http://www.loc.gov/pictures/item/cwp2003000880/PP

time for the battle (who joined 890 men already there under the command of Lieutenant Colonel John E. Tourtellotte. However, the railroad transit was fraught with difficulties – a good indication of the shape of southern railways by **1864**:

> The train, in moving down to Rome, threw some fourteen or fifteen cars off the track, and threatened to delay us till the morning of the 5th, but the activity of the officers and railroad employees enabled me to secure a train of twenty cars about 7 p. m. of the 4th. Onto them I loaded three regiments of Colonel Rowett's brigade and a portion of the Twelfth Illinois Infantry, with about 165,000 rounds of ammunition, and started for Allatoona at 8.30 p. m., where we arrived at 1 a. m. on the morning of the 5th instant, immediately disembarked, and started the train back, with injunctions to get the balance of the brigade and as many of the next brigade as they could carry and return by day-light. They unfortunately met with an accident that delayed them so as to deprive me of any re-enforcements until about 9 p.m. of the 5th.[38]

Allatoona Pass in 1864, looking south. The house to the right and the small brick building in the center are still there today.[39]

---
[38] *War of the Rebellion: Official Records of the Union and Confederate Armies*, U.S. Government Printing Office, 1891
[39] Library of Congress http://www.loc.gov/pictures/item/90716103

By **November 9, 1864**, it was Sherman, not Hood who issued orders to destroy the W&A - from Big Shanty to the Chattahoochee, as he prepared for the March to the Sea.

> In accordance with instructions from Major-General Sherman, commanding Military DIVISION of the Mississippi, corps commanders will have their commands in readiness to march at a moment's notice to commenced the complete destruction of the railroad...From Big Shanty to a point eleven miles south will be destroyed by the Seventeenth Army Corps, and thence to the Chattahoochee bridge by the Fifteenth Corps. The destruction will be most complete, the ties burned, rails twisted, &c., as [has] been done heretofore.[40]

As part of this destruction, the Lacy Hotel (of Great Locomotive Chase fame) was burned to the ground on **November 14, 1864**.

Sherman's March was something new in warfare where a large modern army on purpose destroyed its own supply lines, and decided to live off the land for several weeks. Sherman had experimented with the idea during the Atlanta Campaign when he veered away from the Western & Atlantic Railroad to avoid fighting at Allatoona Pass, thus resulting in the battles of Dallas, New Hope Church, Pickett's Mill, etc. But he eventually returned to the W&A, and set up a supply depot at Big Shanty to prepare for the great battle at Kennesaw Mountain. During the March to the Sea, there would be no supply line for Union troops until they linked up with Union ships in Savannah.

---

[40] *War of the Rebellion: Official Records of the Union and Confederate Armies*, U.S. Government Printing Office, 1891

Ruins of the W&A car shed in Atlanta[41]

On **November 12, 1864**, the destruction of Atlanta began. Sherman ordered everything destroyed except "houses and churches". Anything that could help the Southern war effort was destroyed – railroads, warehouses, manufacturing plants, public buildings, etc. Sherman's chief engineer Orlando Poe was in charge of the destruction, and used battering rams, fire, and explosives. Among the W&A infrastructure destroyed: track, rolling stock, the W&A train shed, and the W&A roundhouse.

---

[41] Library of Congress LC-DIG-stereo-1s01400

Sherman's troops tearing up W&A track[42]

After the War, from the letters of the Boston Daily Evening Traveller correspondent Russell H. Conwell discussed what was left of the W&A:

> All along the Railroad from Ringgold to Atlanta black ruins, old chimneys, broken bridges, and dilapidated fences astonish the eye of the traveler. Ruin! ruin! ruin!...
>
> At Big Shanty, we found nothing but the old blacksmith's shop to mark the place where such a vast army encamped, and where so many poor fellow suffered and died in the hospital. We went

---
[42] Library of Congress, LOT 4164 A, George Barnard photo

upon the hill near the railroad cut, where we last saw Mother Bickerdyke, the Florence Nightingale of the West, caring for the sick in the Army-of-the-Tennessee Hospital. We found there some tent pins and the hewn tree under which so many dead were laid before burial.[43]

With the end of the Civil War in 1865, the rebuilding of the W&A began. On **July 4, 1865, t**he W&A was operational again to Atlanta. On **September 25, 1865**, control of the W&A was returned to State of Georgia.

An **1865** report shows the dreadful condition of the W&A at the time of the end of the Civil War:

> A patchwork of damaged and crooked rails, laid on rotten crossties and or rough poles and other makeshifts, eight miles of track at the upper end was entirely missing and the rolling stock was more nearly fit for the scrap heap than for traffic. (1865 report)

William Tecumseh Sherman later commented on the importance of the W&A to War-time operations, in a letter to the son of Governor Joseph Brown:

> ...the Atlanta Campaign of 1864 would have been impossible without this road, that all our battles were fought for its possession, and that the Western and Atlantic Railroad of Georgia 'should be the pride of every true American' because, 'by reason of its existence the Union was saved'. (William Tecumseh Sherman, 1886, in a letter to Joseph M. Brown, son of the wartime governor)

---

[43] *Magnolia Journey: A Union Veteran Revisits the Former Confederate States*, Joseph Carter, University of Alabama Press, 1974

This 1864 photo shows Union supply wagons near the W&A car shed. A George Barnard photo.[44]

---

[44] LOC http://www.loc.gov/pictures/item/cwp2003000878/PP

Post-Civil War

The General

After the end of the Civil War, the *General* was repaired, and returned to revenue service. It would receive its first numeric designation.

Date	Activity
1865	The Western & Atlantic Railroad is returned to State of Georgia. The *General* is listed as in need of "general repairs".
September 30, 1866	The annual report of W&A for the year ending 9/30/1866 indicates the General had been repaired for $2,887.45, and assigned to freight service[45]
1866	The *General* is assigned locomotive number 39, as it was the 39th locomotive placed in service on the W&A

---

[45] *The General and the Texas*, by Stan Cohen & James G. Bogle

Some data exists regarding the use of the *General* in the years immediately following the Civil War:

Year Ending...	Miles	Repair costs	Cars pulled
9/30/1867	22,300	$759.38	2,712[46]
9/30/1868	19,389	$497.75	2,419[47]
9/30/1869	13,222	$2,260.70	1,040[48]

Reconstruction

In **1870**, Foster Blodgett was named Supervisor of the W&A. Blodgett was a close ally of Radical Republican Governor Rufus B. Bullock. Blodgett fired several hundred W&A employees, and replaced them with his own appointees. William A. Fuller was "discharged for being a Democrat".

---

[46] *Ibid*
[47] *Ibid*
[48] *Ibid*

Governor Rufus B. Bullock[49]

Also in **1870**, the State of Georgia decided that it no longer wanted to be in the railroad business, passing legislation that required the leasing of the W&A (the State of Georgia would continue to own the right of way, as it does today). On **December 27, 1870**, a group led by former governor Joseph E. Brown won the first lease of the W&A. The lease was for 20 years, for $25,000/month.

In the early 1870s, The *General* was completely rebuilt by the W&A, converted to a coal burner with a diamond stack

The Great Kennesaw Route

During the Brown leasing period, the W&A was marketed as the "Great Kennesaw Route", and the "Battlefield Route".

---
[49] Library of Congress LC-BH8266- 1641

Marietta was marketed as a winter resort, and the "Gem city of Georgia".

The Western & Atlantic Railroad runs through Palace Sleeping Cars and through Parlor (chair) Cars, daily, with the N. C. & St. L. Ry., from Nashville to ATLANTA via MARIETTA; and through Palace and Buffet Sleeping-Cars, daily, with the Cincinnati Southern Railway (Queen & Crescent Route), from Cincinnati to Jacksonville, Fla., via MARIETTA and ATLANTA.

There are Sleeping or Parlor Cars on all through trains of the Western & Atlantic Railroad.

The Western & Atlantic Railroad is the only one in the South which runs FOUR THROUGH PASSENGER TRAINS per day each way. Its service is therefore unrivalled.

The Western & Atlantic Railroad is the only one entering ATLANTA from the Northwest which lands passengers and makes all connections in the Union Passenger Depot, and thus saves invalids, ladies, and all others, a long and cold omnibus transfer to the hotels or to other railroads.

The Western & Atlantic Railroad runs FOURTEEN THROUGH AND LOCAL PASSENGER TRAINS per day.

The Western & Atlantic Railroad is the only one running through the beautiful and historic Chickamauga Valley.

The Western & Atlantic Railroad has been termed "The Historic Battlefields Route of America" because it runs through or near the famous battlefields of Lookout Mountain, Missionary Ridge, Chickamauga, Ringgold, Rocky Face, Resaca, New Hope Church, Allatoona, Kennesaw Mountain, Atlanta, and more than fifty other minor conflicts at arms which took place during 1863 and 1864.

The Western & Atlantic Railroad is the one which General W. T. Sherman says "should be the pride of every true American, because by reason of its existence the Union was saved."

The Western & Atlantic Railroad has rock ballast, steel rails and iron bridges.

From **1870-1899**, the *General* began its metamorphosis from being used for revenue service to becoming a national icon. At the time of the Brown lease in **1870**, the *General* was valued at $2,000. Records indicate that the *General* ran 127,886 miles during State of Georgia operations.

Date	Activity
Early 1870s	The *General* is completely rebuilt by W&A, and converted to a coal burner with a diamond stack
1880	The *General* is reassigned number 3, since it was the third oldest locomotive on the W&A at that time. This is the number still worn by the *General* today.

1886	The *General* (and the whole W&A) is converted from 5 foot gauge to 4' 8.5"
1887	Our heroic locomotive rescues stranded passengers near Chickamauga and also pulls a special train for International Convention of Car Accountants
1887-1888	The *General* is rented to Atlanta & Florida RR
1888	The *General* is involved in a Grand Army of the Republic encampment in Columbus, OH. The encampment includes a reunion of Andrews Raiders.
1889	The *General* is displayed at the Society of the Army of the Cumberland meeting in Chattanooga
1890	The *General* undergoes repairs in Atlanta shops

On **Dec. 27, 1890**, the W&A was leased by the Nashville, Chattanooga & St. Louis Railway (NC&StL), although it continued to operate under the Western & Atlantic name until **1919**, when it became the "Atlanta Division of the NC&STL RY". The NC&StL lease was for 29 years at $35,001/month. Essentially, the W&A as an independent entity had ceased to exist in 1890. As the *General* was transferred to the NC&StL, it was labeled "condemned, value $1,500".[50] I

In **1891**, the *General* was retired from service, and temporarily moved to a siding in Vinings, GA. In **1892** it was refurbished by the NC&StL shops in West Nashville and briefly converted back to a wood burner. It began its life as a popular road show locomotive, appear at conventions and expositions around the country.

Date	Activity
1893	The *General* appears at the World's Columbian Exposition in Chicago
1895	The *General* appears at the Cotton States and International Exposition in Atlanta
1897	The *General* is displayed at the Tennessee

---

[50] *The General and the Texas,* by Stan Cohen & James G. Bogle

Centennial Exposition in Nashville

The *General* on a siding in Vinings, GA, with E. Warren Clark in the cab. (Photo courtesy Southern Museum of Civil War and Locomotive History)

Dr. Warren Clark (on cowcatcher) with the General following the 1892 NC&StL overhaul (Collection of Edith Knox; courtesy of Southern Museum of Civil War & Locomotive History)

The Century Turns

In the 20th Century, the *General* would bask in the glow of being the most famous and revered locomotive in America. In **1962**, the *General* would retrace its route from the Great Locomotive Chase under its own steam. Tennessee and Georgia would fight over who owned the *General* (a fight that went all the way to the Supreme Court).

On **May 16, 1901**, the *General* went on "permanent" display at Union Depot, Chattanooga. It would reside here until **1961**, except for various times when it was displayed at conventions and other events. While Union Depot was physically in the State of Tennessee, the land it stood on was owned by the State of Georgia. This would later be a key fact in the legal battle that raged from **1967-1970** over ownership of the *General*.

The *General* in Union Depot, Chattanooga

Date	Activity
1906	The *General* appears at the Grand Army of the Republic (GAR) Annual Encampment in Chattanooga

1927	The *General* appears at the Centenary Exposition of the B&O in Maryland
1933	The *General* appears at the Century of Progress Exposition in Chicago
1939	A resolution is passed in the Georgia Legislature to have the *General* put on permanent display at Kennesaw Battlefield. While nothing comes of this resolution, it is the first shot fired by Georgia towards Tennessee over the ownership of the *General*.
1939/40	The *General* appears at the New York World's Fair

Railroad Exhibit, 1939 World's Fair[51]

Date	Activity
1948	The *General* appears at the Railroad Fair in Chicago
1957	The NC&StL merges into the Louisville and Nashville Railroad (L&N). As a result, all assets and liabilities of the NC&StL are assumed by L&N. This will become a significant legal point over who actually owns the *General* in the late 1960s.
1959	The Stone Mountain Memorial Association proposes to have the *General* put on

---

[51] From the collection of Louise Jones

	permanent display in Stone Mountain; the L&N declines
June 6, 1961	The L&N removes the *General* at night to South Louisville Shops for reconditioning. It is converted to an oil burner, which it remains today.
Feb. 7, 1962	The General operates under its own power for first time since 1914!

1962 Centennial Run of the General

On **April 14, 1962**, the reconditioned *General* ran under its own steam from Tilford Yard in Atlanta to Chattanooga. The run was in commemoration of the 100th anniversary of the Andrew's Raid on **April 12, 1862**. *Trains* magazine (July 1962) estimates that 100,000 people viewed the centennial run of the *General*, including crowds of 10,000 in Kennesaw (where the train was stolen), and 12,000 in Ringgold (where the chase ended).

The trip from Atlanta to Chattanooga took about 8 hours. The *General* is reported to have reached a speed of 50 mph between Ringgold and Chattanooga.

Kennesaw went so far as to erect false storefronts on the west side of Main Street to give the town a fuller and more "old time" feeling. Period dress was *de rigeur*.

Kennesaw (Big Shanty) greets the *General* in 1962[52]

---

[52] Frank Burt Family collection

Kennesaw on April 14, 1962 (Photo by C. Norman Beasley)[53]

---

[53] Courtesy Southern Museum of Civil War and Locomotive History

Return of the General to Kennesaw

After the centennial run of the *General* in **1962**, it was returned to Chattanooga for display in Union Station. The *General* repeated its centennial run under its own steam in **1963**. On S**ept. 17-21, 1966**, the *General* ran under its own steam for the last time near Paducah, KY.

Starting in **1967**, a three-year dispute raged between Chattanooga, TN and the State of Georgia/L&N RR over the ownership of the *General*. The dispute started in February, **1967** when the L&N Railroad agreed to give the General to the State of Georgia. This gesture was probably done to encourage renewal of the lease for the W&A right of way, which was set to expire on **Dec. 27, 1969**.

A resolution accepting the General from the L&N was passed by the State of Georgia on **March 16, 1967**:

> H. R. No. 124-311 (AS PASSED HOUSE)
> By: Messrs. Wilson and Henderson of the 102nd, Howard of the 101st, and Cooper of the 103rd
>
> Urging that the famous steam locomotive known as the GENERAL be returned to the State of Georgia; and for other purposes.
>
> WHEREAS, Mr. William H. Kendall, President of the Louisville & Nashville Railroad Company, has graciously offered to return the famous steam locomotive known as the GENERAL to the State of Georgia; and
>
> WHEREAS, one of the most thrilling adventures in the history of warfare took place on April 12, 1862, during the Civil War, and involved two steam locomotives known as the GENERAL and the TEXAS; and
>
> WHEREAS, this adventure began when a raiding party of Federal soldiers, disguised as civilian passengers on the GENERAL, and led by James J. Andrews, seized the GENERAL at Big Shanty, which is now Kennesaw in Cobb County, Georgia, and steamed northward

with the intention of destroying the railroad so as to sever connections between Atlanta and Chattanooga; and

WHEREAS, the GENERAL was seized by the Federal raiding party while Confederate Captain William A. Fuller, who was the conductor, and the train crew and passengers were having breakfast at Big Shanty; and

WHEREAS, upon realizing that the GENERAL had been seized, Captain Fuller and his men began immediate chase; and

WHEREAS, Captain Fuller and his men began said chase on foot and then used a push-car, a locomotive known as the YONAH, a locomotive known as the WILLIAM R. SMITH, and finally the famous locomotive known as the TEXAS; and

WHEREAS, Captain Fuller and his men exhibited extraordinary courage and determination in this chase; and

WHEREAS, because of such courage and determination the GENERAL was finally abandoned by Andrews and his raiding party two or three miles above Ringgold, Georgia, where it was being overtaken by the TEXAS; and

WHEREAS, after abandoning the GENERAL, Andrews and his raiders fled into the woods while being pursued by Captain Fuller and several Confederate soldiers who had come to his aid; and

WHEREAS, twenty-two of the raiders, including Andrews, were captured by Captain Fuller and the Confederate soldiers; and

WHEREAS, Andrews and seven other members of the Federal raiding party were subsequently executed in Atlanta, Georgia, as Federal spies; and

WHEREAS, the locomotive chase of April 12, 1862, would put the most gifted writer of fiction to task in duplicating this thrilling adventure which is a matter of historical fact; and

WHEREAS, this great historical event has been immortalized in a motion picture entitled "The Great Locomotive Chase".

NOW, THEREFORE, BE IT RESOLVED BY THE GENERAL ASSEMBLY OF GEORGIA that this body does hereby express its deepest appreciation to Mr. William H. Kendall, President of the Louisville & Nashville Railroad Company, for his kind offer to return the GENERAL to the State of Georgia.

BE IT FURTHER RESOLVED that upon there being erected an appropriate structure within the City of Kennesaw, Georgia, which, in the judgment of the State Properties Control Commission will adequately protect and preserve this valuable historic locomotive, the GENERAL shall be located and available to the public view in the City of Kennesaw, Georgia.

BE IT FURTHER RESOLVED that the Clerk of the House of Representatives is hereby authorized and directed to transmit an appropriate copy of this resolution to Mr. William H. Kendall, President of the Louisville & Nashville Railroad Company.

An historical society was formed in the City of Kennesaw on **March 24, 1967** to encourage Governor Lester Maddox to sign the resolution (Stone Mountain and Ringgold were also jockeying for position to receive the General). Below is part of the minutes from the first meeting of the newly formed Big Shanty Historical:

> Several attempts have been made in past years, by citizens of Kennesaw and Cobb County, to have "The General" returned. These efforts were intensified when the movie "The Great Locomotive Chase" was being filmed. These efforts all failed, however, and it wasn't until the 1967 session of the Georgia Legislature, that a determined effort was made again, to secure The GENERAL and place it in a museum near the place from which it had been stolen over a hundred years ago.
>
> The idea was first presented by Representative Joe Mack Wilson, while a heated debate was being waged over the lease of the W&A Railroad, which was built, and is owned by the State of Georgia.
>
> The Cobb County delegation, consisting of Representatives William C. Cooper, J. H. Henderson, Jr., G. Robert Howard, Hugh Lee McDaniell and Joe Mack Wilson, acted as a committee for Cobb County, and supporting the L&N position, devoted their

time and talents in approaching the President of the Louisville and Nashville Railroad (Mr. William H. Kendall) to ask that The GENERAL be returned to Kennesaw, Georgia (formerly Big Shanty) where the "great locomotive chase" had begun more than a century before. With considerable difficulty, these representatives were able to out-maneuver a group of law-makers from Ringgold, Georgia, plus another powerful delegation determined to have The GENERAL at Stone Mountain.

The proposal, House Resolution Number 124 - 311, (a copy of which is preserved on preceding pages) cleared the Georgia House and Senate, only to launch the Cobb Delegation on an even tougher mission - - - that of convincing Governor Lester G. Maddox to sign the resolution. This they accomplished despite heavy opposition from a seemingly more influential group from the Stone Mountain camp.

The Resolution was signed into law the 16th day of March, 1967.
A meeting of interested citizens was called at Kennesaw City Hall.
A meeting of interested citizens was called at Kennesaw City Hall.
Those in attendance at this initial meeting were:

Mayor James Adams (Kennesaw)	C. N. Marsh
Mayor Howard Atherton (Marietta)	W. P. Matlock
Lynda Barron	Stephen C. May, Jr., M.D.
R. T. Beets	J. R. McCollum
Mrs. Marvin C. Brown	Dent Myers
R. L. Butler	Jack Myers
Richard Butler	William S. Newman, III
J. C. Cantrell, Jr.	Barbara Reinagel
Cindy Fitzgerald	L. E. Watts
Lee Garner	Velma Weeks
Charles Harden	Rep. Joe Mack Wilson
Rep. J. H. Henderson, Jr., M.D.	W. B. Wright
Rep. G. Robert Howard	

On **April 5, 1967**, Governor Lester Maddox signed the resolution calling for the return of the *General* to Kennesaw. It would be three more years before the ensuing legal battle was resolved, and almost two years more after that before the *General* was ensconced in the museum in Kennesaw.

Lester Maddox (r) with Joseph W. Parrott, grandson of Jacob Parrott & Wilson W. Brown[54]

| Return of the General to Kennesaw ||
Date	Activity
September 12, 1967	The *General* is en route to Kennesaw to participate in a 3-day festival, when it is stopped at 1:30am by a party led by Chattanooga Mayor Ralph Kelly. The 3-year court battle begins.
Dec. 16, 1967	The *General* is moved to the Louisville shops of the L&N (approved by U.S. District Judge Frank W. Wilson)
Jan. 4, 1969	U.S. District Judge Frank W. Wilson rules that the L&N owns the General
May 21, 1970	U.S. Court of Appeals of Appeals for the Sixth District upholds lower court ruling

---

[54] Photo courtesy Southern Museum of Civil War and Locomotive History

Return of the General to Kennesaw	
Date	Activity
November 9, 1970	The Supreme Court of the United States refuses to overturn a lower court ruling granting ownership of the General to the L&N RR

In **c. 1971**, the Frey family of Kennesaw donated the building and land for the Big Shanty Museum to the City of Kennesaw. On **February 18, 1972**, the *General* was presented to the State of Georgia (accepted by Governor Jimmy Carter) by the L&N railroad, and moved to Kennesaw on a railroad flatcar, arriving around 6:00p. The next day, the *General* was transferred to the back of a truck, and eased into the back of the Big Shanty Museum (now the Southern Museum of Civil War and Locomotive History). Speakers on that dreary February day included Kennesaw Mayor Louis Watts.

The *General* arrives in Kennesaw, February 1972 (Photo by Joe Bozeman)

The *General* waiting to be put into the new Big Shanty Museum (Photo by Joe Bozeman)

The *General* after it was taken off of the flat car, February 1972 (Photo by Joe Bozeman)

On **April 12, 1972**, the Big Shanty Museum (now the Southern Museum of Civil War and Locomotive History) opened to the public in the old Frey cotton mill, 110 years after the Andrews Raid. The *General* had come home to Kennesaw!

April 12, 1972 - Opening day at the Big Shanty Museum, home of the *General*[55]

The *General* at the Big Shanty Museum

---

[55] Courtesy of Southern Museum of Civil War & Locomotive History

89

The General Stamp

On **July 28, 1994**, a stamp honoring the General was released by the USPS. On **July 29, 1994**, a "Second Day Issue" ceremony was held at the Big Shanty Museum (now Southern Museum of Civil War and Locomotive History) in Kennesaw, Georgia. Speakers at the ceremony included Catherine Fletcher (Kennesaw Civil War Museum), Kennesaw Mayor J.O. Stephenson, *General* historian Col. James Bogle, and Kennesaw Postmaster Ralph Brooks.

Colonel James Bogle speaks at the "Second Day Issue" ceremony of the *General* stamp, at the Big Shanty Museum.

The 21ˢᵗ Century

The Southern Museum of Civil War and Locomotive History opened on **March 30, 2003**. The 40,000 square foot Museum is the new home of the *General*. The Southern Museum was built around the Frey Cotton Gin which housed the *General* starting in **1972**, so the *General* has been housed continuously in the same structure for 37+ years.

Opening of the Southern Museum of Civil War and Locomotive History

Descendents of the Raiders gather for the opening of the Southern Museum of Civil War and Locomotive History on March 30, 2003

Appendix: Nashville, Chattanooga & St. Louis and beyond

In **1890**, the Western and Atlantic Railroad ceased to exist as a separate corporate entity, when the Nashville, Chattanooga & St. Louis Railway purchased the lease from the State of Georgia (although the name Western & Atlantic would survive for another 20 years).

In **1919**, the Nashville, Chattanooga & St. Louis Railway renewed their lease for the old W&A right of way for 50 years at $45,000/month.

c. 1908 photo of a NC&StL Railway water tower (left), 19th century railroad shanty (center), and the c. 1908 depot (right), in Kennesaw, GA. (Photo courtesy Southern Museum of Civil War and Locomotive History)

1915 NC&StL water tower (Courtesy Frank Burt family)

In **1957**, the NC&STL merged with the Louisville & Nashville Railroad, and L&N became the new name for the old W&A right-of-way. In **1972**, "The Family Lines" name was adopted to identify the SCL, L&N, CC&O, the Georgia Railroad and the West Point Route.

Finally, on **November 1, 1980**, the CSX Corporation was formed, resulting from the merger of the Chessie System and the Seaboard Coast Line. The CSX operates under a lease from the State of Georgia, on the old W&A today.

Sources

- *Capturing a Locomotive* by William Pittenger (The National Tribune, 1881)
- *Daring and Suffering: A History of the Andrews Railroad Raid* by William Pittenger, 1887
- *Fields of Glory* by Jim Miles (Rutledge Hill Press, 1989)
- *General and the Texas, The* by Stan Cohen & James G. Bogle, Pictorial Histories Publishing, 1999
- *General: The Great Locomotive Dispute, The* by Joe F. Head (Etowah Historical Foundation, 1990)
- *Ghost Trains & Depots of Georgia (1833-1933)*, by Les R. Winn (1995)
- *Great Locomotive Chase As Told By Men Who Made It Happen, The*, edited by Gene Aiken (Historic Press/South, 1994)
- *Great Locomotive Chase or, The Andrews Raid, The* by James G. Bogle (Blue & Gray Magazine, Blue & Gray Enterprises, July, 1987)
- *History of Kennesaw* by Mark H. Smith (Kennesaw Gazette, 1980/81)
- http://www.csx.com/index.cfm?fuseaction=history.heritage
- *Kennesaw (Big Shanty) in the 19th Century* by Robert Jones (2000)
- *Kennesaw in the 20th Century* by Robert Jones (2004)
- *Magnolia Journey: A Union Veteran Revisits the Former Confederate States*, Joseph Carter, University of Alabama Press, 1974
- *Southern Confederacy*, April 15, 1862, Atlanta, GA
- *Western & Atlantic Railroad - Marietta: The Gem City of Georgia*, 1887, Jos. M. Brown, reprinted by Cobb Landmarks & Historical Association
- *Western & Atlantic Railroad, The* by James G. Bogle (unpublished)
- *Western & Atlantic Railroad: An Illustrated Timeline, The* by Robert Jones (2008)

Photos by Robert Jones, unless otherwise noted

A final note on sources: Many of the "facts and figures" that appear in this book, especially on the W&A, came from research done by Colonel James Bogle, and appeared in an unpublished paper by him entitled *The Western & Atlantic Railroad.* As are all students of the *General*, the Great Locomotive Chase, and the Western & Atlantic Railroad, I am indebted to Colonel Bogle for his tireless research in these areas.

The Author on YouTube

There are several extracts of lectures by the author on Civil War topics available on YouTube, including:

Sherman's March: Strategy and Results
(http://www.youtube.com/watch?v=gAcqx0rpWXY)

Sherman's March: The Fall of Savannah
(http://www.youtube.com/watch?v=Iykjb7vA3wI)

Overview of the Great Locomotive Chase
*(*http://www.youtube.com/watch?v=CSJ03W8mlMc*)*

Author singing *"Hold the Fort"*
(http://www.youtube.com/watch?v=5LzWtVXAYAE)

All of these can be viewed in high definition (720p).

The author is available for lectures in the Atlanta/North Georgia area. See http://www.rcjbooks.com/guest_speaker for details.

About the Author

Robert is President of the Kennesaw Historical Society, and Director of Programs and Education for the Kennesaw Museum Foundation. He is also on the advisory board for the Civil War Round Table of Cobb County. He has written several books on Civil War and railroad themes, including:

Battle of Allatoona Pass: The Forgotten Battle of Sherman's Atlanta Campaign, The
Battle of Chickamauga: A Brief History, The
Battle of Griswoldville: An Infantry Battle on Sherman's March to the Sea, The
Bleeding Kansas: The Real Start of the Civil War
Civil War Prison Camps: A Brief History
Famous Songs of the Civil War
Fifteen Most Critical Moments of the Civil War, The
Images of America: Kennesaw
Pennsylvania Railroad: An Illustrated Timeline, The
Reading Railroad: An Illustrated Timeline, The
Retracing the Route of Sherman's Atlanta Campaign and March to the Sea
Top 20 Best – and Worst – Generals of the Civil War, The
Top 20 Civil War Spies and Irregulars, The
Top 20 Most Influential Leaders of the Civil War , The
Top 20 Railroad Songs of All Time, The
Top 25 Most Influential Women of the Civil War, The
W&A, the General, and the Andrews Raid: A Brief History, The

Robert is an ordained elder in the Presbyterian Church. He has written and taught numerous adult Sunday School courses. He is also the author of:

25 Most Important Events in the Post-Apostolic Christian Church, The
25 Most Influential Books in the Post-Apostolic Christian Church, The
25 Most Influential People in the Post-Apostolic Christian Church, The
25 People Who Most Influenced the Music of Christianity, The
A Brief History of Protestantism in the United States
A Brief History of the Sacraments: Baptism and Communion
Crusades and the Inquisition: A Brief History, The
Heaven and Hell: In the Bible, the Apocrypha and the Dead Sea Scrolls
Meet the Apostles: Biblical and Legendary Accounts
Monks and Monasteries: A Brief History
Old Testament Views of the Messiah and Jesus Christ

Origins of the New Testament
Revelation: Background and Commentary
Top 25 Misconceptions About Christianity, The
Top 25 Most Influential Protestants in the United States, The
Top 25 Most Influential Protestants in England, The

Robert has also written several books on "Old West" themes, including:

Death Valley Ghost Towns – As They Appear Today
Ghost Towns of Southern Arizona and New Mexico
Ghost Towns of the Mojave National Preserve
Ghost Towns of Western Nevada
Top 10 Gunslingers and Lawmen of the Old West, The

In 2005, Robert co-authored a business-oriented book entitled *Working Virtually: The Challenges of Virtual Teams*.

jone442@bellsouth.net
rcjbooks.com

Cover: The *General* at the Big Shanty Museum (now Southern Museum of Civil War and Locomotive History).

Made in the USA
Lexington, KY
25 July 2018